Exodus from Egypt

Series editor: Rachel Cooke
Art director: Robert Walster and Jonathan Hair
Consultants: Reverend Richard Adfield; Marlena Schmool
and Samantha Blendis, Board of Deputies of British Jews

First published in 2000 by Franklin Watts

First American edition 2000 by Franklin Watts
A Division of Grolier Publishing
90 Sherman Turnpike
Danbury, CT 06816

Visit Franklin Watts on the Internet at:
http://publishing.grolier.com

Catalog information is available from the Library of Congress
Cataloging-in-Publication Data

ISBN 0-531-14585-9 (library ed.). -- ISBN 0-531-15437-8 (pbk.)

Exodus from Egypt

Retold by Mary Auld

Illustrated by Diana Mayo

W

FRANKLIN WATTS

A Division of Grolier Publishing

NEW YORK • LONDON • HONG KONG • SYDNEY
DANBURY, CONNECTICUT

Long ago, God's chosen people, the Israelites, were slaves in Egypt. The Egyptians worked them hard and treated them badly, and the Israelites cried out to God for help.

God heard their cries. He decided He would free the Israelites from Egypt and take them to their own land. He chose a man named Moses to lead them. Moses would have to persuade Pharaoh, the king of Egypt, to let the Israelites go. But Moses was a poor speaker, so his brother Aaron was asked to talk for him. Moses would tell Aaron what to say, just as God told Moses.

Moses and Aaron went to Pharaoh and said: "The Lord, the God of Israel, says to you: 'Let my people go, so that they may worship me in the desert.'"

But Pharaoh replied, "Who is the
Lord? I don't know him, and I will not
let the Israelites go."

That same day Pharaoh gave orders
to his slave-drivers to work the
Israelites still harder. They already
made bricks, but now they had to
gather the straw to mix into the brick

 6

mud as well. And they had to produce
as many bricks as before.

When the Israelites complained to
Pharaoh, he was furious. "Lazy, that's
what you are — lazy!" he cried. "All
you want to do is go into the desert
and make sacrifices to your Lord.
Now get back to work."

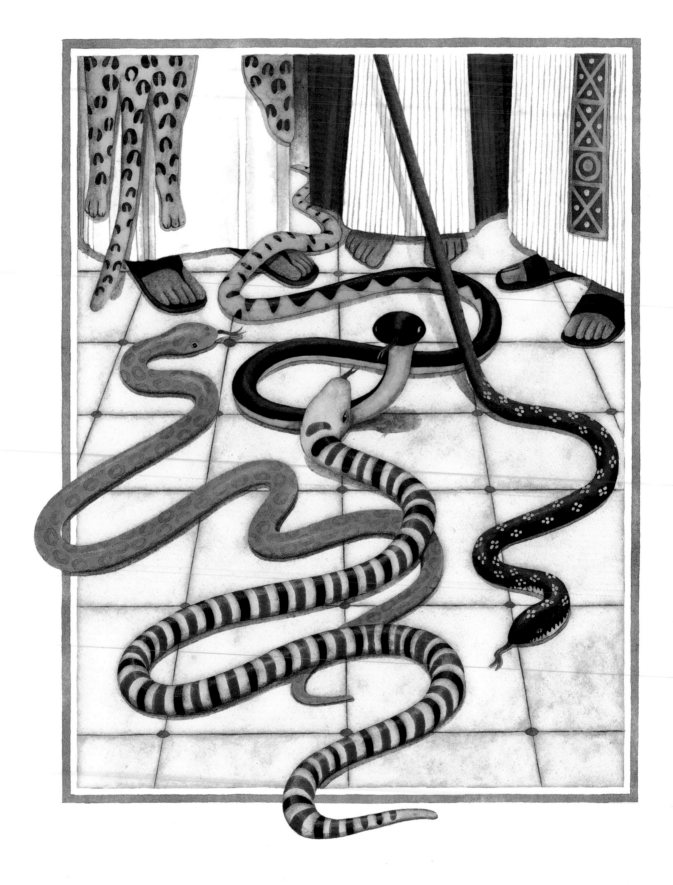

Moses was unhappy. He spoke to God. "Why have you brought trouble on my people? Is this why you sent me?"

God replied: "Go with Aaron again to Pharaoh. Ask again to bring the children of Israel out of Egypt. Pharaoh will not listen. I shall harden his heart, but then I shall show him my power with signs and marvels. The Egyptians will know that I am the Lord."

So Moses and Aaron went again to Pharaoh. This time, to show God's power, Moses told Aaron to throw his staff on the floor. Instantly, it became a snake.

Pharaoh summoned his magicians. Each of them threw down his staff and each staff became a snake. So, even though Aaron's snake swallowed the others, Pharaoh would not listen to Moses, just as God had said.

Now God sent ten great plagues. First, He told Moses to go to Pharaoh again. "Meet the king by the edge of the Nile. Aaron must stretch his staff out across the river. Its waters will turn to blood — there shall be blood throughout the land."

Moses and Aaron did as God commanded. As Pharaoh and his

courtiers watched, Aaron struck the Nile with his staff and its water turned to blood. All the fish in the river died, and the water smelled so bad that the Egyptians could not drink it. But again Pharaoh's magicians could perform similar tricks. Pharaoh returned to his palace and refused to change his mind.

A week passed and Moses went again to Pharaoh. "The Lord says: 'Let my people go or I will plague your whole country with frogs. They will come into your palaces and your bed. They will climb all over you.'"

And, when Pharaoh still refused God's demand, the frogs came and covered the land. Pharaoh's magicians called up frogs as well, but this time Pharaoh was frightened. He summoned Moses and said, "Beg your God to remove the frogs, and I shall let your people go."

Moses did as Pharaoh asked. The frogs died and were piled into heaps, and the land reeked of them. But when Pharaoh saw that the problem was gone, he changed his mind. The Israelites must stay in Egypt.

So God sent a new plague — a plague
of lice that crawled over all the Egyptian
people and their animals. Pharaoh's
magicians could not copy this marvel.
"This is the finger of God," they told their
king. But Pharaoh refused to listen.

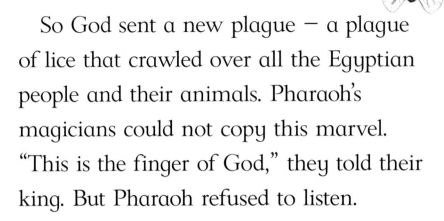

And Moses said to Pharaoh, "The Lord says: 'Let my people go or I shall send a plague of insects. They will cover your houses, but the Israelites' homes will remain untouched.'" The great swarms came, and Pharaoh said he would let the Israelites go if Moses would remove the insects. But when the insects were gone, Pharaoh again went back on his word.

And so it continued – God sent plague after plague, and each time, Pharaoh would agree to let the Israelites go. But as soon as God removed each plague, Pharaoh's heart would harden and he would break his promise, just as God had said.

There was a plague that killed all the Egyptians' cattle and sheep, then another that caused boils and ulcers to break out on all the Egyptians and their animals. Pharaoh's magicians had so many boils that they could not stand before Moses.

Next came terrible storms: Moses raised his staff to the sky, and God sent down hailstones mixed with thunder and lightning. The stones battered the Egyptians' barley and flax, but left the Israelites' crops untouched.

The Egyptians were becoming
desperate. "Let the Israelites go," the
courtiers said to Pharaoh. "Can't you
see Egypt is ruined?" But when
Pharaoh spoke to Moses, he offered to
let only the Israelite men leave Egypt,
not their women and children.

 17

In reply, Moses stretched out his staff
across the land. This time God sent a
swarm of locusts that ate everything
that the hail had not destroyed: the
Egyptians' wheat, the fruit in their
trees. Nothing green remained.

Once again, Pharaoh agreed to let
the Israelites go if God would remove

the locusts, and once again, when the
locusts had gone, he broke his word. So
God sent a great darkness over Egypt,
which lasted three days. No one could
see anyone else or leave his place. God
gave only the Israelites light to see by.

But still Pharaoh would not agree to
Moses' demands.

Now God spoke to Moses: "I shall bring one more plague on Egypt. After that, Pharaoh will let you go. Tell the Israelites to prepare for a meal: Each household shall kill a lamb. They shall put some of its blood around the doorways of their houses. Then they shall roast the lamb and eat it. That night I shall pass through Egypt and kill every firstborn son. But where I see blood on the door, I shall know to pass over that house. Death will not strike the Israelites as it does the Egyptians."

And Moses told the Israelites all that
God had said, and they did as He
commanded. And at midnight on that
day, God struck down all the firstborn
sons of Egypt, from the firstborn of
Pharaoh, who sat on the throne, to the
firstborn of the prisoner, who was in the
dungeon. A loud cry rose up from the
Egyptians, for there was not one house
without someone dead.

Pharaoh called Moses and Aaron in
the middle of the night. "Get up and
go from among my people, you and
the Israelites. Go worship the Lord as
you have asked!" And all the Egyptians
urged the Israelites to leave.

So the Israelites took their belongings
and set out from Egypt. There were
about six hundred thousand men on

foot, along with women and children.
They took their flocks and their herds,
and on their shoulders they carried
dough without any yeast, because they
did not have time to prepare the bread
properly. And they journeyed toward
the Red Sea, with God ahead to guide
them — by day in a pillar of cloud and
by night in a pillar of fire.

 23

Now Pharaoh began to regret his decision. He had his chariot made ready and, with a vast army, set out in pursuit of the Israelites.

The Israelites were camping by the shores of the Red Sea when they saw the Pharaoh's armies. Terrified, they cried out to God. Moses reassured them.

"God will save you. You will never see the Egyptians again. Just stand firm." And, following God's orders, Moses raised his staff and stretched out his hand across the sea. The waters parted and the Israelites went across the sea on dry land, a wall of water on their right and a wall of water on their left.

Pharaoh, with all his soldiers, chariots, and horses, followed. But God made the wheels of the chariots stick, and it was difficult for them to move forward. The Egyptians began to panic.

When all the Israelites had safely crossed the sea, Moses turned and stretched out his hand across the water. The walls of water broke down and flooded together again, covering Pharaoh and his entire army. All the Egyptians drowned.

Finally, the Israelites knew they were safe. They had seen God's power and they had faith in Him and His servant Moses. Miriam, Moses' sister, took a tambourine and, with all the other women, danced and sang in praise of God, who had led them out of Egypt.

About This Story

Exodus from Egypt is a retelling of part of Exodus, one of the books that make up the Bible. The Bible is the name given to the collection of writings that are sacred, in different forms, to the Jewish and Christian religions. Exodus is the second of 39 books in the Hebrew Bible, Tanakh, or Christian Old Testament. As one of the first five books of the Bible, Exodus is also part of the Torah, the most sacred text of the Jewish religion.

Leaving Egypt

Exodus means "the going out." It refers to the Israelites' journey out of Egypt, which is the key event in the book of its name and the climax of this retelling. The Exodus probably took place near the start of the 13th century B.C., during the reign of the Pharaoh Ramses II (1290-1223 B.C.). The Israelites (or Hebrews) had originally come to Egypt about 400 years before this to avoid famine in Canaan. They were then a large family, headed by Jacob (called Israel by God). Initially the Egyptians had welcomed them, but over the centuries, as the Israelite numbers increased, the Egyptians had begun to feel threatened by them and forced them to be their slaves.

Plagues and Marvels

The Israelites were God's chosen people, and they prayed to Him to free them from Egypt. With Moses and Aaron's support and through the extraordinary plagues and marvels, God gave the Israelites their freedom. Before this event, the Bible tells us how God had generally shown Himself to His people through one person. Now, in the pillars of clouds and fire, He chose to lead them on their journey Himself. He even parted the Red Sea — the Sea of Reeds in the original Hebrew — for them. Never could the Israelites have felt so close to God or more bound together as His people.

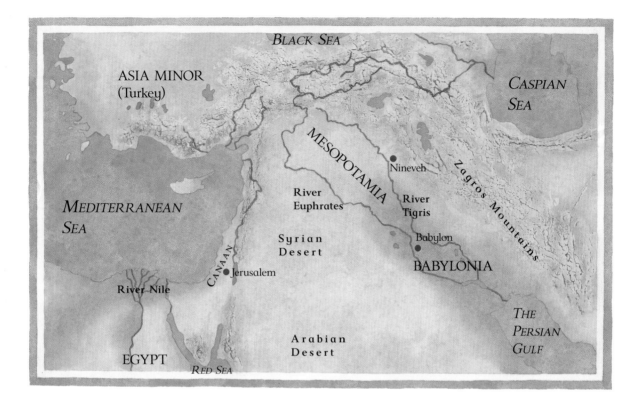

The Passover

After leaving Egypt, the Israelites wandered through the desert for forty years before they eventually reached Canaan. But they never forgot God's actions. The Exodus was one of the first and most important events in Jewish history. To this day, Jews everywhere remember it in the festival of Passover (Pesach). This name recalls how God passed over the houses of the Hebrews when He struck down the Egyptians' firstborn sons. Pesach takes place over eight days every spring. During it, the Jews eat only unleavened bread (bread without yeast) called matzo. This reminds them that the Israelites left Egypt in a hurry and did not have time to make bread properly. On the eve of the festival, a Jewish family eats a special Seder meal, which includes lamb, to remember the meal on the eve of the tenth plague, and bitter herbs to remember the bitterness of slavery in Egypt.

Useful Words

Boil A boil is a swelling under the skin caused by buildup of poisonous pus. A boil becomes an ulcer when the skin breaks and pus begins to ooze out.

Desperate If people are desperate, they are without hope and in extreme discomfort or unhappiness. They will do anything to end their pain.

Israelites Also known as Hebrews, the Israelites were an ancient people from the Middle East among whom the Jewish religion began. They took their name from their ancestor Jacob, whom God called Israel, which means "to strive to understand God." After leaving Egypt, the Israelites settled in Canaan and formed the nation of Israel.

Lice Lice are wingless insects. They are parasites, which means they live on the bodies of other animals, including people.

Locust A locust is a type of insect, much like a large grasshopper. Locusts gather together in huge swarms, eating (and destroying) any plants they find.

Magician A magician is someone who knows about and performs magic. In ancient times, people took magic very seriously and believed that it could explain many things in life they did not understand. A magician was seen as a wise and knowledgeable man, not just someone who did tricks.

Marvel A marvel is something amazing or extraordinary that you would not expect to happen in your everyday life.

Ruined Something is ruined when it has been completely destroyed and damaged beyond repair.

Sacrifice A sacrifice is a gift or offering made to God to worship or give thanks to Him. The sacrifice may be food or money, or it can be an animal such as a goat, which is killed. Animal sacrifice used to be part of some Jewish ceremonies. Today, people usually use the word sacrifice to describe giving up something important to them for someone else's sake.

Staff A staff is a long, straight walking stick.

Worship To worship God is to praise Him and to show your love for Him. There are many ways of worshiping God, including prayers and hymns.

Yeast Yeast is used in baking bread. It is made up of minute fungi. (Fungi are a group of living things.) A mixture of yeast, water, and sugar is added to bread dough to make it rise and expand.

What Do You Think?

These are some questions about *Exodus from Egypt* to ask yourself and to talk about with other people.

How would it feel to be a slave?

Why do you think Pharaoh made the Israelites work harder after Moses asked for their freedom?

Why was Moses unhappy with God?

Why do you think God made sure Pharaoh would not listen to Moses?

What do you think the difference was between God and the magicians?

Why do you think Pharaoh kept changing his mind?

How do you think the Egyptians felt when all their firstborn sons died?

What do you think it felt like to walk across the Red Sea?

What do you think the Israelites felt when they gained their freedom?

 31

4/0'

ML